UNCLE FLEETWOOD AND HMS DASHER

Lieutenant Fleetwood Elwyn Price

UNCLE FLEETWOOD

AND

HMS DASHER

BY

TERENCE WHIPPY

COUNTRY BOOKS

Published by Country Books
Courtyard Cottage, Little Longstone, Bakewell, Derbyshire DE45 1NN
Tel: 01629 640670
e-mail: dickrichardson@countrybooks.biz
www.countrybooks.biz
www.sussexbooks.co.uk

ISBN 978-1-910489-66-6

DEDICATION

For Phillipa Broadway (Fleetwood's grand niece)
To help her generation to remember.
And for
Fleetwood's sister Primrose Whippy (my mother)

Printed and bound in England by 4edge Ltd., Hockley, Essex

Contents

Acknowledgements

Many members of my family have helped me to put this book together. My grateful thanks go to Fleet's daughter Monica (now sadly deceased) who gave me access to her personal photo album and other documents. Also thanks to my friend John Steele who has kindly let me use many facts and figures from his excellent books on the demise of HMS Dasher. The National Archives has been another source of very interesting information. Stephen Lloyd my local MP for Eastbourne and Norman Baker the former Lewes MP have both at various times written to the MOD on my behalf trying to prompt them into revealing more details on the tragedy but the replies received shed no new light on the situation at all. Thanks also go to Geoff Bridger for help with the photos. One strange aspect to all this is that neither the British Legion nor the CWGC wanted to help in any way and the Royal Naval Association thought it may be political so they also declined to help.

I just hope that at some point in the future the books of John Steele and this small volume inspire someone else to delve deeper into the sinking of HMS Dasher and the "missing bodies."

Early Years

Fleetwood (henceforth referred to as Fleet) Elwyn Price was born on January 20th 1901 two days before the death of the long serving Queen Victoria. His formative years were passed in the reign of Edward Vll to a background of hansom cabs, gaslights and Sherlock Holmes serials in the Strand magazine.

He was the second son of Charles Alfred and Eliza Jane Price of Dartmouth Park Avenue, Tottenham who had married in 1897. They had five children altogether Lawrence who was killed during the First World War on the western front in 1918, Fleet, May, Primrose (my mother), and Phyllis. Unfortunately Charles their father passed away in 1910 of consumption.

Eliza Jane and Charles Price

After leaving Tottenham Grammar School in the summer of 1915 Fleet went to work for the London and South Western Bank as his brother Lawrence had done two years before .Following his seventeenth birthday in 1918 he decided the time had come to join the army and do his "bit". Unfortunately by this stage of the war the forces wanted proof of age and 18 was the age the army enlisted men. His brother Lawrence had written to him from the western front a couple of days before he was killed in action on April 25th of that year advising him there were "young soldiers battalions "that took and trained 17 year olds to be ready for service at 18 but we can only presume he did not like that idea. After trying various branches of the armed forces he found the navy would take him on as an apprentice (to train as an officer). He duly signed on for this and was posted to HMS Knight Templar which was at Devonport making ready to sail for Halifax, Nova Scotia.

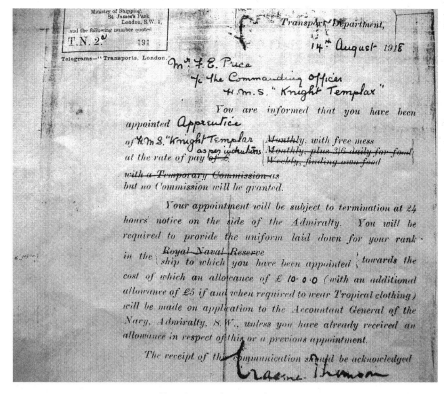

Fleet's appointment letter

HMS Knight Templar was an armed merchant cruiser taken over by the navy for the duration of the war. She was 11,370 tons and armed with a 6" gun on the forecastle, two 6" guns on the saloon deck amidships a 6" gun on the poop deck and two howitzers in the forewell. The ship had been launched in 1905 and had been built by Charles Connell & Co, of Scotstoun. She had had an eventful war in December 1917 she was in the harbour at Halifax, Nova Scotia when a munitions ship bound for England blew up near by the crew immediately joined in the rescue attempts. In the spring of 1918 she was damaged by a torpedo in the Atlantic but managed to limp back to port for repairs.

When the vessel sailed out of Devonport en route back to Halifax on the 17th August 1918 Fleet got his first taste of naval life. It took 12 days for the convoy, the ship had joined, to reach its destination as it could only go as fast as the slowest ship, also the constant

Midshipman Fleetwood Price

zigzagging to confuse u-boats added time to the voyage. HMS Knight Templar had by this stage of the war been treated to "dazzle camouflage" as seen in the accompanying photo which was another ruse to try to ward off u-boat attacks by confusing their range finding equipment.

After arriving at Halifax on 29th August 1918 and loading ready for the return journey she sailed to Sydney Nova Scotia to await the rest of the convoy and on the 7th September started the long trip back to England. Apart from the steering gear failing causing a three hour stop in mid ocean for repairs the 12 day journey was uneventful and on the 20th September berthed at Greenland dock London. After a few days discharging her cargo, coaling and taking on ballast she left London en route to Plymouth to meet another convoy to escort once again to Halifax and set sail on 8th October. She arrived on the 25th of the month after much zig-zagging and heavy seas to contend with… the entry in the log book for the 20th reads "high confused seas, vessel labouring heavily".

The ship started the return journey on Armistice Day 11th November 1918 this was to be a very rough trip as for five days she was caught in a strong gale and some of the ship's equipment was lost overboard. For four days the log book reads "Vessel rolling heavily at times and shipping water fore and aft" on the 17th she had to stop engines for repairs the work took two hours with the ship pitching and rolling dangerously at times. She passed Beachy Head on 26th and berthed at Gravesend on the 27th completing what proved to be her last convoy duty.

After unloading Knight Templar stayed in port until the evening of 13th December when she departed for Liverpool and moving a day later to Lewis Wharf, Birkenhead. The crew then started dismantling all Royal Navy equipment from the vessel this took many days with the guns being removed on the 21st December. On 31st December 1918 the crew were discharged and the ship decommissioned from naval service. Fleet was then posted for nine months to HMS Sunhill which was moored on the Thames as an instructional establishment. He was demobbed in August 1919 thus bringing to an end his first taste of naval life.

MIDSHIPMAN NICHOLSON R.N.R. H.M.S. KNIGHT TEMPLAR 1918

PERRY ?. BLANT BONSFIELD . PRICE

PARRY

"Midshipman"

HMS Knight Templar

World War Two

Between the wars Fleet worked for the London based paper manufacturing company Spicers. He married Olive in 1928 and they had two daughters Monica and Thelma. Just after the start of the Second World War Fleet again volunteered for active service and successfully went before an Admiralty Selection board on June 4th 1940. He was then sent to Greenwich for a few months refresher course. In the late autumn of that year he was posted to HMS Montclare an armed merchant cruiser which was undergoing a refit to accommodate more anti aircraft guns. Before the war SS Montclare had been a passenger ship owned by Canadian Steamships Ltd. On 28th August 1939 she was requisitioned by the Admiralty and converted to an armed merchant cruiser, after being modified to naval standards she became HMS Montclare in October 1939.

When Fleet joined the ship in November 1940 he was appointed gunnery officer and became responsible for two depth charge throwers, five 5 inch guns, three 4 inch guns and two Lewis machine guns. After this extensive refit she eventually left Liverpool for Halifax, Nova Scotia on May 1st 1941. Armed merchant cruisers such as Montclare were a throw back to the first world war when there were no aircraft carriers to escort convoys on there journeys. Land based aircraft from Britain or Canada could not reach the middle of the Atlantic and there was a gap of about 300 miles with no hope of air cover. At the start of WW2 there were still no carriers available to accompany the convoys so the more modern and faster of the merchant ships were fitted with guns and weapons to ward off attacks from hostile aircraft, ships and submarines. Usually one or two of these vessels would escort each convoy with possibly a royal navy destroyer as well.

Grosvenor Gardens House,
Victoria,
London, S.W.1.

C.G.E.1.

25ᵗʰ May, 1940.

Dear Sir,

With reference to your offer of services, you are invited to appear before an Admiralty Selection Board at Grosvenor Gardens House, S.W.1. (near Victoria Station) on Tuesday June 4ᵗʰ at 10.30 A M

I am to point out that all appointments require that officers should be physically fit and generally that they are sufficiently fit to be employed at sea. Should you not be up to this standard I suggest that you should inform me accordingly, as it would probably be a waste of your time to appear before the Selection Board.

Officers selected will, in any case, have to undergo medical examination.

No expenses in connection with this visit can be refunded.

It is requested that you will bring references and B.O.T. certificate with you.

I am, Sir,

Your obedient Servant,

Rear-Admiral.

President, Admiralty Selection Board No.5.

Fleet's Admiralty Selection Board Letter

14

HMS Montclare in her later wartime role as a submarine support ship

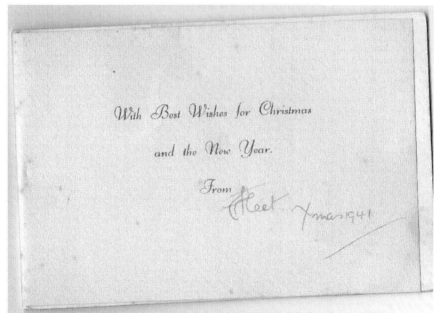

A Christmas card from Fleet to his sister Primrose

Whilst Fleet served aboard her the movements of the ship were as follows.

1ˢᵗ May 1941	Left Liverpool for Halifax, Nova Scotia.
6ᵗʰ May 1941	Arrived at Halifax.
14ᵗʰ May 1941	Sailed from Halifax.
16ᵗʰ May 1941	Anchored at Bermuda.
18ᵗʰ May 1941	Left Bermuda to join convoy.
27ᵗʰ May 1941	Left convoy.
30ᵗʰ May 1941	Arrived at Halifax.
31ˢᵗ May 1941	Left Halifax for Boston.
1ˢᵗ June 1941	Arrived at Boston.
3ʳᵈ June 1941	Into No.3 dry dock Charleston Navy Yard.
21ˢᵗ June 1941	Left Boston for Halifax.
24ᵗʰ June 1941	Arrived at Halifax
27ᵗʰ June 1941	Left Halifax to join convoy across the North Atlantic.
7ᵗʰ August 1941	Anchored off Repave (Iceland)
10ᵗʰ August 1941	Left Repave to escort a convoy back to Halifax.
18ᵗʰ August 1941	Arrived at Halifax.
2ⁿᵈ September 1941	Left Halifax.
5ᵗʰ September 1941	Arrived at Bermuda.
11ᵗʰ September 1941	Left Bermuda.
14ᵗʰ September 1941	Arrived back in Halifax.
13ᵗʰ October 1941	Left Halifax for return to Bermuda.

15th October 1941   Arrived at Bermuda.

20th October 1941   Returned to Halifax.

22nd October 1941   Arrived at Halifax to rendezvous with another convoy.

24th October 1941   Left Halifax for England.

After arriving back in England on October 30th the ship berthed at the Empire Jetty in Falmouth and stayed there until March 10th 1942 when she moved to Devonport. This was followed by a move to Southampton on March 31st. Here many of the guns were removed along with the ammunition and general stores. In the middle of April with this work complete the ship was laid up prior to being converted to a submarine depot ship and the crew discharged.

Fleet with one of his gun crews on HMS Montclare in the Gulf of Maine
May 20th 1941

Fleet in his cabin on Montclare

HMS Dasher

With HMS Montclare being laid up Fleet was now posted as gunnery officer to HMS Dasher which was in the Brooklyn Navy Yard being converted from a cargo ship to a "fleet escort carrier ".

Early in 1940 the Moore McCormack Lines Shipping company of America had commissioned the Sun Shipbuilding Company of Pennsylvania to build four new passenger/cargo ships for plying between South America and New York mainly to carry bananas and a few passengers. These were all requisitioned as they were launched for conversion to escort carriers. They became HMS Biter, HMS Avenger, HMS Dasher and the fourth was retained by the US Navy and was named USS Charger. Dasher was launched as the "Rio de Janeiro" on April 12th 1941 and then became BAVG4 whilst the work of converting her was taking place. Due to be completed in July 1942 Fleet and the new crew had been transported to New York arriving in June of that year to give them a few weeks to familiarise themselves with the ship.

On Thursday July 2nd 1942 at 10.00 in the morning the commissioning and naming ceremony for HMS Dasher was held on board but due to inclement weather this took place in the ships hangar instead of on the flight deck as planned. This was followed by Divine service at 10.15 and at 10.25 the ship's company was addressed by Rear Admiral Marquand USN and Admiral French RN. In the evening there was a handing over dinner for the officers and local dignitaries. One of the first entries in the ship' log for July 4th 1942 reads "up spirits – first issue" the first rum issue on the ship the entry is initialled by Uncle Fleet.

With the work complete and the rest of the crew on board Dasher sailed out of he Brooklyn Navy Yard on July 25th 1942 passing under the famous Brooklyn Bridge and going on to Long Island Sound to take on some swordfish aircraft. The first deck

The launching of the Rio De Janeiro which became HMS Dasher

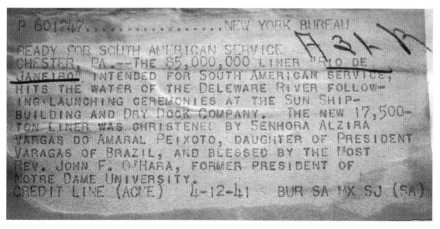

Information on the back of the photo of the launching of the Rio De Janeiro

landing was completed satisfactorily at 11.30 but unfortunately at 12.41 an aircraft crashed on deck and at 14.10 another one overshot the flight deck and crashed into the sea luckily both pilots survived these mishaps. HMS Dasher anchored for the night in Oyster Bay Long Island. By the 29th July she had moved up the Hudson river to Hoboken Pier No.2 but at 9.45 on that date the

Fleet

log book records "explosion in the engine room" apparently caused by a backlash in the water heater boiler. Three civilian workers were slightly burned. This proved to be a minor problem as the ship's engines were giving the chief engineer many problems and it took another two weeks to rectify them although these same problems plagued the vessel throughout its eight months of service life. So with the engines declared serviceable and four swordfish from 837 Squadron on board she joined convoy HX205 at Boston and sailed via Halifax to Britain on 24th August 1942. The convoy arrived in the firth of Clyde on 10th September and Dasher went immediately to a shipyard in Greenock to be brought up to royal navy standards. Before all these modifications could be carried out the ship was again needed for convoy duties, to make the ship more stable 1,200 tons of iron ballast was put into the bilges, my mother had told me that Fleet had told her that Dasher was like "a pea on a drum" in choppy seas.

The duties she was needed for were to escort the troop and supply ships on their way to take part in Operation Torch the landings in North Africa that were intended, after defeating the Vichy French in Tunisia, to attack the Africa Corps from the west while the eigth army was doing the same from the east. Although this operation had sound military reasoning behind it there were other political pressures which persuaded the allies to go ahead with it as Stalin was urging Churchill and Roosevelt to open another fighting front to relieve the German pressure on the Russian front. Also it was designed to show the American public that their troops were making a contribution to the war in Europe. Some of the British aircraft were given American markings so as not to antagonise the Vichy French forces, we were attacking, too much as we had previously sunk their main battleships to stop them falling into German hands. Dasher and the convoy arrived at Gibraltar on 3rd November to refuel and take on fresh water and late on the evening of the 6th November along with her sister ship HMS Biter she left harbour to provide air cover for the landings. While the ship was standing off Oran in North Africa and her aircraft were giving support to the attacking troops she had to move position by some miles due to an enemy submarine being reported in the vicinity. Unfortunately this made it difficult for the aircraft returning to her some ran out of fuel, some managed to make it back to the coast and a couple landed on another carrier. With the troops all landed and making good progress the convoy of transport ships set off back to Britain escorted by one of Dasher's sister ships HMS Avenger. Half way through the voyage in the middle of the night Avenger was torpedoed by a u-boat the torpedo struck her amidships igniting the bomb store and the ship blew up and sank within a few minutes there were 12 survivors out of a crew of just over 500.

In a file relating to the sinking of Avenger released in 2012 at the National Archives at Kew I came across an internal admiralty memo shown below. It says Officers and crews of similar ships are calling this class of vessels "death traps" and this talk must stop. There were many of the Dasher's crew who thought she was an unlucky ship. I think one of the problems was due to the ships being built to peacetime specifications and now they were being asked to carry out tasks as warships.

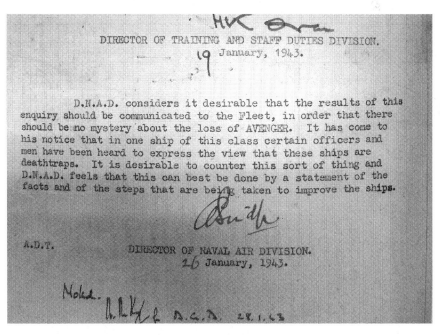

Naval death traps memo

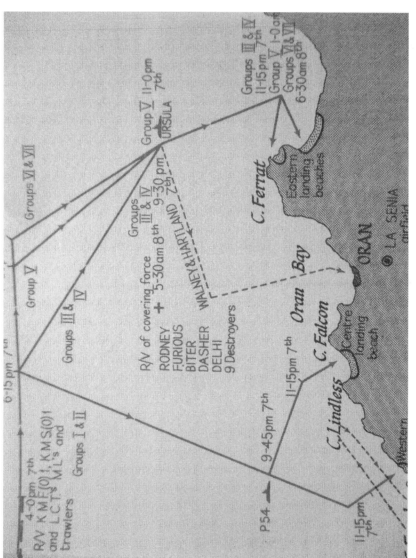

"Operation Torch" attack at Oran

When Dasher arrived back in England on November 20th she immediately went into Liverpool's Alexandria Dock for more safety modifications. Work was carried out strengthening the area around the bomb store to stop the same thing happening to Dasher as had happened to Avenger. Engine problems and a persistent strong smell of petrol were investigated and an air defence control room was fitted. All this work took about two months to complete but gave the crew time to get some well earned leave.

Fleet's grand niece Phillipa Broadway in front of Brooklyn Bridge under which Dasher steamed on 25th July 1942.

Two views of HMS Dasher in the Gulf of Maine waiting for convoy HX 205 to Britain to form up .It proved to be the only Atlantic convoy she took part in

HMS Dasher

Officers of Dasher and the US Navy at the handover dinner in New York.
Fleet is in the centre at the back.

BEXHILL 1938

Fleet on holiday before the war he was only 38 when this photo was taken so it was not surprising some of his shipmates called him "Pops".

In the Diary of 804 squadron (one of Dasher's two aboard the other being 891 squadron) there is an account of what happened to the unit whilst taking part in Operation Torch. It seems to have been written a little while after the event and is a bit gung ho even for the Fleet Air Arm. Here is an exert from the document now kept at the National Archives at Kew;

"On the fateful morning of Nov. 8th the C.O, Hancock, Goodfellow, Crossman, McEvoy and McKennan flew off at 5.30, Crossman touched the sea with his tail but managed to remain airborne (he doesn't remember a thing about it). The merry little party had a great time thrashing up the odd cyclist but saw nothing else and eventually decided to return to the ship. Needless to say they never found the ship and tried to return to Oran. S/Lt McLennon failed to make it and bailed out over the sea and was fortunately picked up by a destroyer. S/Lt Goodfellow did very well and forced landed intact on the dried up bed of a salt lake from where he flew back to Dasher the following afternoon. The C.O., Hancock, McEvoy and Crossman crash landed near Oran successfully writing off all the cabs (aircraft). Crossman was promptly jailed by the French and had a very easy time watching U.S. Rangers being slaughtered with machine gun fire, the C.O., meanwhile did some invaluable reconnaissance work for a U.S. army general in a borrowed hurricane. The flyers eventually rejoined Dasher at Gib. in a varied assortment of ships. McEvoy unfortunately took passage home aboard the Avenger and was lost when she was torpedoed. On 22nd of Nov. HMS Dasher docked at Liverpool and landed the squadron who proceeded to Dombristhle, the C.O. flying the only hurricane."

Fleet at his gunnery control position on Dasher

On the bridge of Dasher giving instructions to crew on the flight deck.

Convoy JW53

At the end of January with these modifications and repairs carried out the ship went back to Greenock to be re-supplied for her next assignment which was to be escorting a convoy round the top of Norway and well into the Artic Ocean to keep clear of German aircraft stationed in the Nordic countries and on to Murmansk in Russia. With her aircraft from 816 and 837 squadrons on board she set sail in rough seas to Scapa Flow and a few days later on to Seidisfijord to rendezvous with convoy JW53. On February 16th with the weather worsening the convoy left for there destination but after only two days were met with a force eleven gale and mountainous seas, waves almost 60ft high, wind speeds that reached 75 mph and a temperature of minus 25 Fahrenheit. So severe was the storm that HMS Sheffield had a gun turret smashed by the storm and even HMS Belfast (now moored in the river Thames) had to seek shelter off Iceland, six merchant vessels of the convoy also turned back. HMS Dasher, to quote John Steele in his book *The Secrets of HMS Dasher* "having been built to ply American coastal waters, on the expedition to Murmansk proved ill equipped". Many of the crew felt sure the ship would capsize any minute and the gale force winds were blowing the life boats and life rafts off there fixings into the sea ,below decks things were as bad. The swordfish aircraft on the flight deck were lost overboard and the swordfish and sea hurricanes in the hangar broke free and crashed into each other, in the torpedo storage area some had broken and were rolling from side to side with the ships motion Things got so bad that eventually the Captain declared the flight deck and the hangar out of bounds to all crew.

Much of the following is taken from the 'WAR DIARY OF THE COMMANDER IN CHIEF, HOME FLEET FOR THE MONTH OF FEBRUARY 1943'

Feb.16th 1943 Force 'A' comprising of DASHER screened by IMPULSIVE, BLANKNEY and LEDBURY left Scapa for Seidisfijord. At the same time Belfast left Loch Ewe for the same destination she was one of over 20 escort vessels for the 29 ship convoy.

Feb.18th 1943 BLANKNEY and LEDBURY arrived at Seidisfijord the former having sustained weather damage in the strengthening gale. DASHER and IMPULSIVE were unable to enter the harbour due to the state of the weather and proceeded with SCYLLA and four destroyers to Akureyri. BELFAST had hove to and rode out the dreadful conditions off Seidisfijord with SHEFFIELD who had had her "a" turret roof ripped off and washed overboard.

Following HMS Belfast in convoy JW53

At anchor off Halvfijord, Iceland waiting to be escorted back to Scotland
after sustaining storm damage

Feb.19th 1943 DASHER and IMPULSIVE still lying off Akureyri as they were still unable to enter the harbour due to the conditions.

Feb.20th 1943 With the storm conditions starting to abate DASHER and IMPULSIVE arrived at Akureyri both with weather damage DASHER was found to have a huge split in its port side about 60ft long caused by the massive waves she had encountered.

Feb.21st 1943 After the damage she had sustained was assessed it was decided she would have to return to Scotland for repairs.

Feb.22nd 1943 Escorted by BLANKNEY and LEDBURY, DASHER left Akureyi for Scapa Flow where her escort was taken over by NEWARK and WELLS for the onward journey to Dundee.

March 1st 1943 Arrived at Dundee and "taken in hand for weather repairs"

March 20th 1943 With repairs carried out and a hull inspection at

Rosyth she left for Scapa escorted by INGLEFIELD and ORWELL.

March 21st 1943 Arrived at Scapa.

March 22nd 1943 Left Scapa in the company of BLANKNEY for the Clyde.

March 23rd 1943 Arrived in the Clyde.

After a few days of restocking supplies, spares and ammunition she steamed out into the Clyde to give the pilots of the newly arrived aircraft a chance to familiarise themselves with the taking off and landing procedures of the ship. In a few days when up to operational efficiency Dasher was due to join Western Command and some reports suggest she was going to be part of a task force to find and attack the feared German battleship Tirpitz. On the 27th March after exercising was over for the day the captain announced over the tannoy that shore leave in Greenock would be granted to all off duty personnel.

At about 4.40pm with the ship preparing to return to harbour there was an almighty explosion and as the war diary laconically records ...

March 27th 1943 Dasher sank after an internal explosion whilst exercising off the Clyde.

Of the 527 crew members aboard 379 lost their lives. Fleet is understood to have been picked up by HMS Capriceuse alive but died of his wounds soon after his rescue, his body being taken to Greenoch for burial.

When the explosion occurred survivors say they saw the lift platform that brought the aircraft up from the below deck hangar fly straight up in the air for at least 50ft with the force of the blast. Within eight minutes, although one account I found gives the time as 3 minutes, the ship had settled lower in the water and sunk stern first.

Signal saying Dasher sank in three minutes

The Aftermath

Immediately after the tragedy a number of ships including two coastal vessels Lithium and Cragsman and HMS Capriceuse raced towards the pall of smoke from the burning fuel oil and the aviation spirit that marked the spot where Dasher had sunk. Many of the sailors were pulled from the water but unfortunately a lot did not survive the spreading flames. Twenty three bodies were brought ashore and buried 13 in Ardrossan cemetery, 7 in Greenoch and one each in Frizington, Mearns and Paisley. The 379 missing crew members are commemorated on memorials at Plymouth, Lee on Solent, Portsmouth, Chatham, Liverpool and Runnymede.

On the 30th March 1943 just three days after the tragedy HMS Archer had arrived and the Naval authorities started an inquiry into the sinking on board. The inquiry after taking evidence from many of the survivors came to the conclusion that the ship blew up due to petrol and/or aviation spirit fumes being ignited. All survivors were then instructed never to refer to the incident again under threat of court martial.

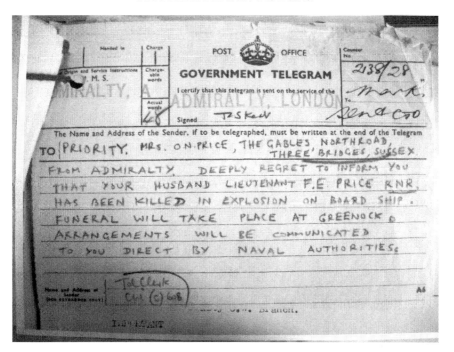

The first Fleet's wife Olive knew of the death of her husband was on receiving this telegram a few days after the tragedy, with the help of the naval authorities she was able to travel up to Greenock for his funeral.

Fleet's headstone in Greenock cemetery.

Fleet's Medals

Top row: WWI   British war medal   Victory medal

Bottom row: WW2   1939-1945 Star   Atlantic star   War medal

THEY WERE NEVER TOLD

THE TRAGEDY OF HMS *DASHER*

THIS MEMORIAL IS
DEDICATED TO
THE OFFICERS AND MEN
WHO PERISHED WHEN
H.M.S. DASHER,
AN ARCHER CLASS
AIRCRAFT CARRIER,
SANK ON 27th MARCH, 1943
"WE WILL REMEMBER THEM"

JOHN STEELE & NOREEN STEELE

Fleet's photo on the cover of John Steele's informative book

Subsequent Years and the search for answers

After many years searching for information on the demise of HMS Dasher whilst idly reading the *Daily Mail* one day in 1995 I came across a review titled "The Tragedy of HMS Dasher" by an author named John Steele. With the help of the *Daily Mail* news desk I contacted him to find that he lived in Ardrossan and from his front room he can look out towards the Isle of Arran and see the site of the tragedy in the river Clyde.

This was a revelation to me as whilst I had been amateurishly and unhurriedly researching the subject of the sinking I was now in touch with a diligent and meticulous researcher who had published a number of books on the subject. Over the next few years we kept in contact with each other exchanging ideas and information and to my surprise he kindly put a photo of my Uncle Fleet on the cover of one of his books. We both agreed that there were three main unanswered questions with regard to the sinking of Dasher.

The first being what caused the ship to blow up in such a spectacular way, various theories have been explored enemy action by aircraft or submarine have been ruled out. An aircraft coming in to land at too lower altitude and striking the gap between the stern of the vessel and the flight deck was a possibility. Another idea put forward was that she hit a mine, other theories have been put forward but until it can be proved otherwise we will have to go along with the conclusion of the court of inquiry which considered the most likely cause was the ignition of fuel vapour.

The second unanswered question was why if 379 men were lost in a river estuary (albeit five and a half miles wide at this point) were there only 24 bodies recovered and buried in various cemeteries. All the buried sailors were identified which to me is rather strange as it is known the fuel oil and aviation spirit caught fire shortly after the sinking. Some of the fatalities surely would have been burnt beyond recognition and dog tags of this era were made of compressed fibre so they would have been consumed by the fire as well. As the ship went down so quickly we could understand if about two thirds of the sailors went down with the ship but even that figure still leaves well over a hundred bodies unaccounted for. It is known that the road north out of Ardrossan along side the Clyde was closed for almost three weeks immediately after the sinking as it was the area the bodies were most likely to come ashore.

In 2012 John Steele obtained a statement a former ARP volunteer who was 17 years old at the time and became a fighter pilot later in the war:

"As a voluntary member of the ARP, I and a number of other ARP personnel drove ambulance trailers to the north shore beach Ardrossan. On arrival we could see bodies laying on the beach the uniforms were badly contaminated with black oil. We placed the bodies on our ambulance trailers and drove them to a building near Ardrossan harbour. Every time we removed bodies from the beach there would always be about six bodies each time. We removed bodies from the beach on many occasions but it did not happen every day. We were always assisted in this task by Royal Naval personnel from the local naval base. The ambulance trailers were towed by cars. Some of the trailers carried four bodies and some carried six. When we were alerted to remove Dasher bodies from the beach we ARP volunteers always arrived with either two or three trailers to convey the bodies to the temporary mortuaries.

Initially we stored the bodies in a building opposite the local newspaper office in Ardrossan. When the building we were taking them to was overflowing we were ordered to collect the Dasher bodies and take them to a small building in nearby Saltcoats, this small brick building was soon overflowing as well and the bodies were taken to Kilwinning another nearby town. There they were placed in a brick building which was in a field. The field was in Stevenson Road, Kilwinning. After these three temporary mortuaries were full, out of respect they were all collected and taken to a prominent building in Glasgow Street Ardrossan. This building was Castlecraigs.

The bodies were laid out on the large dance floor."

When asked how many bodies he assisted in moving he replied "at least 50, there would be at least this number as each day we were involved in removing them we were removing about six bodies each time".

The third unanswered question is why was there so much secrecy surrounding the sinking of HMS Dasher. Once again various theories have been put forward. One being that Britain was very short of carriers to escort convoys at this period of the war and did not want the enemy to know we had lost one. Another was regarding Operation Mincemeat (the man who never was) some, admittedly inconclusive, evidence points to the body used in this operation was a casualty from Dasher. The authorities would have us believe that a middle age tramp living rough in London could be mistaken for a dashing 35 year old Major from the Royal Marines. The submarine HMS Seraph put the body in the sea off Huelva, Spain on the 29th April 1943 just over a month after the sinking of Dasher. The original body had been in cold storage since early in the year and would not have been able to fool a competent pathologist. Some quarters think the tragedy was hushed up so no details of it could be connected to this audacious plan. I have heard that early in April 1943 that HMS Dasher and Operation Mincemeat were discussed at a meeting between the Chiefs of staff and Winston Churchill but I can not locate any minutes to this meeting.

In the late nineties it was realised that the plot in Ardrossan cemetery where the sixteen Dasher bodies were buried was only half used and as the cemetery was considered full this seemed a bit odd. The line of CWGC headstones all faced one way in line abreast, behind them was a six foot strip of apparently unused land. Approaches were made to North Ayrshire Council who had jurisdiction over the cemetery but the then solicitor to the council put many obstacles in the way of an investigation of the plot. The first obstacle he put in the way was to say it was prohibited under the Burial Act (Scotland) 1875 but when I found a copy of the act online he could not tell me which part of the act he was invoking. He then told us we would have to contact the coroners office for permission it was then pointed out to him we did not want to dig up any corpses but just establish if any Dasher casualties were there or not. After a couple of years of letters, emails and phone calls it was agreed aground radar survey could be undertaken.

This was duly carried out by GUARD Archaeology then a department of Glasgow University the project being managed by respected battlefield archaeologist Dr. Tony Pollard. Unfortunately this survey proved to be inconclusive and owing to the nature of the ground the readings from the instruments showed discrepancies in the soil which could be natural or man made. The conclusion from the report suggested the only way to settle the matter was a test excavation. So two years later after another round of letters, emails and phone calls North Ayrshire Council agreed to a limited excavation to clear this matter up once and for all.

GUARD archaeology once again had the task in 2012 and this time the project manager was John Atkinson. A trench six metres by one metre and half a metre deep was excavated but the team found no sign of soil disturbance in the different strata's and concluded the ground had not been disturbed for any sort of burial. This meant we were back to square one and would have to pursue other avenues to try and locate the "missing" bodies from HMS Dasher.

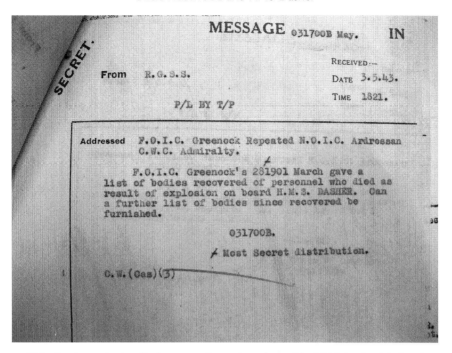

This signal was in the Dasher casualty packs released in 2012 by the National Archive. The "further list of bodies" unfortunately cannot be found

NAME   Fleetwood Elwin PRICE

(a) General conduct.
(b) Of temperate habit.
(c) Professional ability.
(d) Personal qualities.

(e) Leadership.
(f) Intellectual ability.
(g) Administrative ability.
(h) Ability in handling ship.

(i) Fit for more important sea command.
(j) Suitable to specialise.
(k) In what capacity.

(l) Whether recommended for promotion. (Immediate, Accelerated, Ordinary Course or not.)

APPOINTMENT AND DUTY	DATE OF S. 206	(a)	(b)	(c)	(d)	(e)	(f)	(g)	(h)	(i)	(j)	(k)	(l)
MONTCLARE S.206 Gunnery Control	8.40 9.41	Sat	Yes	5	5	5	7	6	—	— No	—	—	O.C. —
MONTCLARE S.206 Control Officer.	9.41 4.42	Sat	Yes	5	5	5	7	6	—	No	—	—	O.C. —
DASHER	8.42 2.43	Sat	Yes	3	6	3	4	3	—	—	—	—	No

MONTCLARE S.206 Gunnery Control — Captain Spreckley. A very reliable officer, but does not know very much of the seamanship side of his work as he has done little sea time. He is quite good at the administrative part of his work. He takes charge of men well, but is familiar with them.

MONTCLARE S.206 Control Officer — Captain Bayley. A steady and reliable officer with a good manner. Good mixer and pleasant messmate. Over 40 and has been 17 years away from the Sea. He has forgotten his navigation and has done no O.O.W. at sea in MONTCLARE. He does not himself feel he is still competent to do O.O.W. at sea.

DASHER — Cmdr. Lentaigne. This officer has been retired from the R.N.R. for a great number of years. He is in habit and movement older than his age would suggest. He tries hard but learns slowly. He has little recollection of the seamanship he learnt when a young officer at sea. Would be better suited in a shore appointment. He is trustworthy but slow.

This appraisal document came from Fleet's service record suggesting he would be more suited to a shore posting as he had been away from sea duties for around 20 years

From   S J Spear

ROYAL NAVY
FLEET HEADQUARTERS

Office of the Naval Secretary
Room G10 (MP G2)
Fleet Headquarters. West Battery
Portsmouth
Hampshire
PO2 8BY

Mrs J Harvey
9 Nicholson Gardens
Heeley
Sheffield
S8 9ST

3 APRIL 2006

Dear Mrs Harvey,

Thank you for your recent letter in which you refer to Operation Mincemeat. the deception operation that involved using the body of an unidentified man in a plan to mislead the axis powers about allied invasion plans in the Mediterranean.
Recent research has indicated that the body used was in fact John Melville, a sailor serving on HMS Dasher.

Thank you for writing

Yours sincerely

A letter from the Admiralty indicating the body used in "Operation Mincemeat" was from HMS Dasher.

Commander R. Mike Crosley's excellent book "They Gave Me a Sea fire" gives a very good insight into carrier life for Fleet Air Arm pilots. He started off flying from HMS Biter but was posted to Dasher for the ill fated JW53 convoy to Russia. The following extracts from his book show Dasher was not a happy ship and there seemed to have been a constant smell of petrol during her service life.

Page 82; Biter was always an efficient and happy ship. Our Captain,"Wings" in the Courageous when she sank, was Connolly Abel-Smith. We were lucky with our Captain and crew. Others were not; notably Dasher.

Page 91; (Operation Torch) Dasher could only make about 12 knots because of her engine trouble. There was a terrible smell of petrol everywhere down below and no one was allowed to smoke on board. We asked one of the junior engineers, who came down to the wardroom for lunch-complete with sweat rags, cotton waste in his overall belt and a dirty, anxious face-what was going on. He said that the "Bloody diesels had blown another pot" and one engine was only giving half power. This explained why the ship was jumping a foot in the air at about a 100 times a minute.

Page 96; In February 1943 , Jacky Sewell called us into his office and asked for volunteers for an operation. We all volunteered but only six were needed. So the C.O., Dougy, Norman Goodfellow, Murdoch Tait, Jimmy Crossman and I flew aboard the dreaded Dasher. The date was 13th February and it was probably a Friday.

Once we had landed on board we learned that we, and some of 891 Squadron who were already on board, were en route for Iceland. We were to be the fighter cover for JW53 Russian convoy. The Ops. Officer on board Dasher pointed out that, sadly, Avenger could not be with us. As if we didn't know.

Things had not improved on board since we had left her at Oran. Still the greasy overalls in the wardroom, the terrible smell of aviation fuel, no water in the cabins. The weather too was awful and allowed no flying.

We sailed with 28 freighters. Then we ran into the worst storm for ages – a force 11 'Severe Storm'. By the time we had reached half way to Iceland, six freighters had turned back, the cruiser Sheffield had had a complete gun turret roof removed by the seas breaking over her and we in Dasher were shipping it green (sea) over the flight deck and into the hangar and had lost two men overboard. The six Hurricanes lashed down on the flight deck were dripping salt water and I, for one, was prepared to be clapped in irons before I flew them.

Down in the hangar all chaos reigned. There were four Hurricanes in the roof of the hangar, as spares. They were slung on wires without wings. They had worked loose and were butting each other, propeller spine against propeller spline, burring the spindles over as they crashed together. Below them on the hangar deck, the lashings on our Hurricanes had had to be tightened to such an extent that they had collapsed the oleos. Oil from them was leaking out onto the hangar making it into a skating rink. A complete 18 inch American torpedo had broken adrift and was washing to and fro in the water in the forward lift well. A five gallon tin of aircraft dope with its lid off was leaving a trail as it rolled in time with the torpedo. Although all aircraft had drained tanks, a strong smell of AVGAS (aircraft fuel) as well as dope pervaded. I suppose a single spark could have set the whole thing off.

Page 97; Barely maintaining steerageway and head to the wind, the ship would occasionally fall off into the hollow of a huge wave. She would then roll through ninety degrees, broadside on. Down below, it was no more difficult to walk up the fore-and-aft passageway walls than it was to walk up the passageway deck itself. Sleeping and eating were impossible. There was nothing for it but to hang on to something solid and, like Jonah, wish for the day.

That evening the storm had eased somewhat so I thought I would make my immobile Wren a Hurricane 'penny'. This was a copper penny, cut, bent and polished to the shape of a Hurricane. I had just found a workshop with a vice and had started sawing out the penny with a hacksaw when the ship gave an immense heave. The huge steel workbench came off the side of the bulk-head and smashed me back against an engine packing case behind me. I escaped only because I happened to be pushed back into a hip sized indentation in the engine itself. I decided against any more workshop do-it-your self and retired to my bunk where I wedged myself in for an hour or two.

Later, I lurched, wide legged and aching, to the wardroom. There, not to be beaten by the elements, were some other good sailors, Norman and the C.O. They told me, with there glasses at 45 degrees and without spilling a drop, that the ship was coming to bits. There was a half inch gap between wind and water for 30 feet along the ship's port side. It opened and closed every time the ship rolled or heaved, and let in about a ton of water everytime. The ship's galley fires were already out and the ship's company were on cold rations. We were retiring to Seydisfiord on the west coast of Iceland to assess the situation. Few of the ship's company realised this because the Tannoy system was also out of action. Later that evening, the RN ship's Senior Engineer came into the wardroom and described the crack still further, saying that you could see the entire convoy through it when it opened. He also announced that because two men had fallen off ladders which had become unwelded as they climbed down them, and had drowned, the Captain had ordered the duty party to assemble in the welldeck with 14 pound ballpeen hammers to knock off any of the hand holds or ladders which remained. The well deck was filled with rusty iron in no time at all.

Next morning, with the storm abated, we dropped our pick (anchor) in Seydisfiord in 40 fathoms, using all the ship's cable end to end. We then brought up some of the better looking Hurricanes onto the frosty deck and changed their fuel, checked r/t, oleos (shock absorbers on the aircraft undercarriage) and engines and sprayed them with fresh water inside and out to get rid of the salt. As this immediately turned to ice, they were taken down below again to melt. Jacky Sewell and some others of us had fun on the deck tractors, towing them about and sliding in ice rinks of frozen green100 Octane, spilled from our tanks. We looked ashore at the black and white misty mountains and the cold, ice-strewn sea between, and we hoped that we would not have to fly or force land or bale out.

As Dasher was once again quite useless, we managed to

retrieve our 80 fathoms of cable after two hours of heaving in, and set course back to Scotland. Four days later Jacky, Norman, Bannister and I flew ashore in the only four flyable Hurricanes, determined at all costs to get airborne even if our engines were only firing on half their cylinders.

Page 98; When we had all landed and were having a nervous drag, the Petty Officer rigger of Station Flight handed me my parachute bag out of the gun bay and told me that the aileron control lines were twisted. The C.O. heard my reply and looked at me in silence for a moment. But when I told him that taking the aircraft was the lesser of two evils and that Dasher was the other one, he agreed to take no further action.

Page 99; During the last days in March 1943, we and our `chummy' Squadron 891, were ordered to carry out some deck landing practice. This was for the benefit of the new boys who had just joined. The only ship available for deck landings was the dreaded Dasher. She was back at Scott-Lithgow's in the Clyde where she had just completed further engine and flight deck machinery repairs when we returned to Hatston we had to leave Maurice Bannister in Dasher's sick bay as he was too sick to fly. Shortly afterwards we heard he had been killed, learning later that Dasher had been torpedoed off the Clyde. Then we heard she had blown up of her own accord without any assistance from the Germans. We believed the last news. We could easily guess why. Much later, I met Lt/Cdr (A) Brian 'Blinkers' Paterson, MBE, DFC, RN, the batsman aboard Dasher when she blew up. He said that someone smoking had touched off the petrol vapour in one of the compartments below. He was batting an aircraft into land at the time, when a great flame shot into the air all around him. HE immediately dived 60 ft over the side. As he always wore a Mae-West even in the shower- he floated high out of the water and was picked up. He told us that when he had come to in the water astern of the flaming Dasher he could see hundreds of her crew jumping over the side straight into the black smoke and red flames of the burning petrol, where they were swallowed up and burned alive, unable to swim faster than the spread of burning petrol on the water.

Page 215; Nothing else worked properly in Dasher either. The radar, the ops room, the r/t, the water supply, the compressed air supply, the petrol supply, (it was contaminated with water half the time) and even her aircraft.

Final Thoughts

The tragic sinking of HMS Dasher illustrates the dire straights Britain was in at this stage of the war. This class of ship was totally unsuited to the role it was given, some even unkindly called them Woolworth carriers, Woolworths were a chain of shops selling cheap items in those days. HMS Dasher's sister ship HMS Biter did however survive to the end of the war after extensive modifications. The main reason for the desperate need for escort carriers was the problem of air cover for the Atlantic convoys. In the early years of the war aircraft from neither Britain or Canada could patrol the middle of the Atlantic due to their fuel capacity so in mid ocean there was a corridor over three hundred miles wide where convoys were without there vital air cover. It could be said that the reason for the sinking being covered up was so we did not embarrass the Americans for their substandard work on these ships but this is one of a number of theories.

With regard to Operation Mincemeat later made into a film called "The Man Who Never Was" referred to earlier in this book, this was a plan to deceive the Germans into thinking the Allies were going to attack Sardinia and not Sicily, their actual target, by the depositing of a body with false information on it off the coast of Spain where many German agents were known to operate from. This was organised by a group set up to mislead and confuse our enemy's known as the Twenty Committee or the XX committee and often referred to as the Double Cross Committee. At one point in the war James Bond creator Ian Fleming was with this unit. The question is why the organisers of this deception would drive hundreds of miles to Glasgow from London in early 1943 with a body to meet submarine HMS Seraph which had come right round the top of Scotland to the Clyde when other more southerly ports were much nearer. The most likely explanation is to obtain a body from Dasher which had sunk a couple of weeks earlier. The Royal Navy has now admitted the body came from Dasher naming him as John Mellville RN. and a memorial service for him was held in 2004 on the current HMS Dasher (a patrol vessel) in the Mediterranean. The Germans did actually fall for this ruse and did in fact move some troops to Sardinia from Sicily but the enemy still holding the island gave the allies a very hard time before its eventual capture.

I suppose I could be accused of having some sort of "conspiracy theory" about the Dasher incident but I will always think it a very peculiar situation that all those bodies could disappear without a reasonable explanation. In wartime some events obviously have to be hushed up for fear of giving help to the enemy but just how long should they remain secret.

So there we are this is all the information I have been able to glean concerning the service life of my Uncle Fleet the second of my Uncles to die in a World War. It seems especially sad in view of his assessment on a previous page   indicating he would be posted to a shore establishment in the not too distant future. In those days it was considered your duty to sign up to fight for your country and I am very proud that he did as did thousands of his contemporary's.

Terence Whippy

September 2018
Eastbourne

DADDY'S LAST LEAVE. 1943.

This very poignant photo from the personal album of Fleet's daughter Monica
I feel is a fitting way to end my tribute to Uncle Fleetwood.

Sources

Personal family documents and photos.

The Secrets of HMS Dasher By John Steele and Noreen Steele

The American Connection to the Sinking of HMS Dasher
       By John Steele and Noreen Steele.

They Gave Me A Seafire By Commander R. Mike Crosley, DSC, RN.

National Archives;
ADM 358/3214 HMS Dasher Casualty Pack.
ADM 358/1512 HMS Dasher Casualty Pack.
ADM 53/116919-20 Inquiry into the Sinking of HMS Avenger.
ADM 115721   HMS Dasher Log Book July 1942
ADM 115722   HMS Dasher Log Book August 1942
ADM 115723   HMS Dasher Log Book September 1942
ADM 115724   HMS Dasher Log Book October 1942
ADM 115725   HMS Dasher Log Book November 1942
ADM 115726   HMS Dasher Log Book December 1942
ADM 117310   HMS Dasher Log Book January 1943
The Log Books for February and March 1943 are believed to have gone down with the ship.
ADM 199/631 Western approach Diaries.
ADM 207/8   804 Squadron (Fleet Air Arm) Diary